Marshal Josip Broz Tito: The Lif

By Charles River Editors

Tito

About Charles River Editors

Charles River Editors is a boutique digital publishing company, specializing in bringing history back to life with educational and engaging books on a wide range of topics. Keep up to date with our new and free offerings with [this 5 second sign up on our weekly mailing list](), and visit [Our Kindle Author Page]() to see other recently published Kindle titles.

We make these books for you and always want to know our readers' opinions, so we encourage you to leave reviews and look forward to publishing new and exciting titles each week.

Introduction

Tito and Eleanor Roosevelt

Josip Broz Tito (1892-1980)

"No country of people's democracy has so many nationalities as this country has. Only in Czechoslovakia do there exist two kindred nationalities, while in some of the other countries there are only minorities. Consequently in these countries of people's democracy there has been no need to settle such serious problems as we have had to settle here. With them the road to socialism is less complicated than is the case here. With them the basic factor is the class issue, with us it is both the nationalities and the class issue. The reason why we were able to settle the nationalities question so thoroughly is to be found in the fact that it had begun to be settled in a revolutionary way in the course of the Liberation War, in which all the nationalities in the country participated, in which every national group made its contribution to the general effort of liberation from the occupier according to its capabilities. Neither the Macedonians nor any other national group which until then had been oppressed obtained their national liberation by decree. They fought for their national liberation with rifle in hand. The role of the Communist Party lay in the first place in the fact that it led that struggle, which was a guarantee that after the war the national question would be settled decisively in the way the communists had conceived long before the war and during the war. The role of the Communist Party in this respect today, in the phase of building socialism, lies in making the positive national factors a stimulus to, not a brake on, the development of socialism in our country. The role of the Communist Party today lies in the necessity for keeping a sharp lookout to see that national chauvinism does not appear and develop among any of the nationalities. The Communist Party must always endeavour, and does endeavour, to ensure that all the negative phenomena of nationalism disappear and that people are educated in the spirit of internationalism." - Tito

The World War II era produced many leaders of titanic determination, men whose strengths and weaknesses left an extraordinary imprint on historical affairs. The struggle between massively divergent ideologies, exacerbated by huge social changes affected by the world's technological metamorphosis into the machine age, catapulted some individuals unexpectedly onto the world stage.

Josip Broz Tito, better known to history as Marshal Tito, was undoubtedly one of these figures. Originally a machinist, Tito leveraged his success in the Communist Party of Yugoslavia (CPY) and a number of extraordinary strokes of luck into dictatorial rule over Yugoslavia for a span of 35 years. World War II proved the watershed that enabled him to secure control of the country, leading an ever more powerful army of communist partisans against both the Germans and other Yugoslav factions. During the war, SS leader Heinrich Himmler himself begrudgingly stated, "He has really earned his title of Marshal. When we catch him we shall kill him at once... but I wish we had a dozen Titos in Germany, men who were leaders and had such resolution and good nerves, that, even though they were forever encircled, they would never give in."

During his reign, Tito managed to quash the intense national feelings of the diverse groups making up the Yugoslavian population, and he did so through several methods. He managed to successfully play the two superpower rivals, the United States and Soviet Union, off against each other during the Cold War, and in doing so, he maintained a considerable amount of independence from both, even as he additionally received foreign aid to keep his regime afloat. All the while he remained defiant, once penning a legendary letter to Joseph Stalin warning the Soviet dictator, "To Joseph Stalin: Stop sending people to kill me! We've already captured five of them, one of them with a bomb and another with a rifle... If you don't stop sending killers, I'll send a very fast working one to Moscow and I certainly won't have to send another."

Never afraid to use political murder when expedient, yet simultaneously outgoing and good-humored to those around him, Tito created a unique and unusual state between the Western democracies and the Eastern Bloc. Only with his death did the fabric of his "national communist" state tear asunder and age-old identities reassert themselves, bringing about a period of intense conflicts that produced a new equilibrium with ethnically-based successor states that cracked up the state he once led.

Marshal Josip Broz Tito: The Life and Legacy of Yugoslavia's First President examines the life of one of the 20th century's most influential leaders. Along with pictures of important people and places, you will learn about Tito like never before.

Marshal Josip Broz Tito: The Life and Legacy of Yugoslavia's First President
About Charles River Editors
Introduction
    Chapter 1: Tito's Early Life
    Chapter 2: World War I and Revolution
    Chapter 3: The Versailles State
    Chapter 4: World War II
    Chapter 5: Tito's Yugoslavia
    Online Resources
    Bibliography
Free Books by Charles River Editors
Discounted Books by Charles River Editors

Chapter 1: Tito's Early Life

"In the most trying hours, through dismal nights and endless interrogations and maltreatment, during days of killing solitude in cells and close confinement, we were always sustained by the hope that all these agonies were not in vain, that there was a strong and mighty country, however far away, in which all the dreams for which we were fighting had been fulfilled. For us it was the homeland of the workers, in which labour was honoured, in which love, comradeship, and sincerity prevailed." - Tito

Originating in Kumrovec, a Croatian village in the shadow of Cesargrad Castle, Josip Broz Tito lived in one of the small town's best houses, that of his parents Franjo Broz and Marija Javeršek. Though his forefathers had built up a relatively large holding of 15 acres and bequeathed him a horse and cart, Franjo Broz found himself in an untenable situation as cheap foreign grain pushed down farm income. He took to drink, and progressive alcoholism only made the family's success melt away faster. Tito himself, in his later surprisingly frank and humorous autobiography, described his parents and the decline of the Broz fortunes: "My father was a wiry man with black curly hair and an aquiline nose. [...] Going to the villages across the Sutla, Franjo became acquainted with a sixteen-year-old Slovene girl called Marija [...] She was a tall, blonde woman, with an attractive face. [...] A hard life awaited my parents. [...] When the debts became intolerable, the soft and good-natured Franjo gave it up and took to drinking, and the whole family burden fell upon my mother, an energetic woman." (Dedijer, 1953, 12-13).

Janez Novak's picture of Tito's birthplace

Born on May 7th, 1892, the future Marshal Tito attended school sporadically. Though he enjoyed education and received commendations from his teachers when he attended his classes, Josip faced opposition from his parents, who believed schooling was useless compared to farm work. Reversing truancy's usual pattern, Tito went "truant" from home to attend school.

Outside of school, Tito proved adventurous, restlessly energetic, and combative. He learned how to be an adept rider at an early age and showed immense fondness for dogs, particularly his favorite pet, a sheepdog named Polak. This animal guarded the younger Broz children reliably and lived to the age of 16.

He also led the local boys in raids on orchards and similar activities, usually playing the part of leader due to his daring and extreme energy. He participated in playful skirmishes simulating the 1573 attack on Cesargrad Castle by Matija Gubec's rebels, with the boys decorating their hats with rooster feathers in the same manner as the bellicose Croatian peasants of some 300 years before. The castle still had a sinister reputation, since although the peasants seized it and killed the bailiff, Baroness Barbara Erdody escaped to return later with fresh troops and slaughter hundreds of the rebels. Tito recalled, "Three centuries later [...] whenever as children we awoke at night, our mother threatened that the Black Queen of Cesargrad would take us away if we did not go back to sleep at once." (West, 2012, 26).

History repeated itself in 1903 with a brief, minor rebellion against the Austro-Hungarians. Then 11 years old, Tito watched the local people tearing down Hungarian flags in protest over a new tax. Soldiers soon arrived to restore Austro-Hungarian rule, and a quartet of Hungarian soldiers received a billet in Franjo Broz's house for four weeks.

As Tito reached his early teens, Franjo Broz wanted to send him overseas to the United States in search of fame and fortune, but poverty prevented him. When he reached the age of 15, Tito went to the town of Sisak, where his soldier cousin Jurica Broz found a job for him as a waiter at a cafe. Tito only stayed at the cafe long enough to save some money, whereupon he set out to find work more suited to his tastes.

Fascinated by railroads and locomotives, Tito tried to find work on a train but failed, so in order to satisfy his craving for mechanical work in some fashion, he enrolled for a three-year apprenticeship with Master Nikolas Karas, a local locksmith of Czech extraction. The job suited Tito, though he sometimes neglected it in his newly discovered passion of reading adventure novels – including Sherlock Holmes stories by Sir Arthur Conan Doyle – and history books: "Josip enjoyed his three years as an apprentice. The work was hard, but he liked it. He liked the smell of oil, the whir of the lathes and drills and the sparks which flew from the molten metal. He liked, above all, the feeling that he was making something." (MacLean, 1957, 9).

The huge Karas found Tito, late in his apprenticeship, neglecting a running drill (which broke) in order to read a Sherlock story. The Czech punched his Croatian apprentice in the face, prompting Tito to run away and join the workers at a brickyard. The police found him almost immediately and threw him in prison for breaking his apprenticeship agreement, but Karas sent him a large meal, then appeared in person to secure Tito's release, after which he finished his apprenticeship without incident.

Tito read his first socialist newspaper, *Slobodna Reč*, in 1909, and when he finished his apprenticeship in 1910 he moved to Zagreb (then named Agram), where he joined the Metal Workers' Union. The young Croatian showed great dedication to the union, attending meetings or demonstrations, and paying his back dues promptly whenever he found work after a period of involuntary unemployment.

Initially, Tito's personal ambition did not extend beyond buying himself fashionable clothing, a fixation undoubtedly due to his frequent raggedness as a child. He saved up a considerable sum from his first independent work to purchase the fanciest suit available for a triumphant return home at Christmas. However, shortly before the holiday trip, he returned from work to find the door of his tiny apartment forced open and his expensive tailored suit stolen, never to be retrieved.

Low-cost American grain exports badly damaged the Croatian economy at the time, forcing Tito to travel from place to place in search of work. His skill and Union membership ensured that he never remained without a paying job for an excessive length of time. He eventually found relatively stable work at a metalworking factory in Kamnik. At this time, Tito also joined a patriotic gymnastic club, "Soko" or "Falcon," though less because of its anti-Habsburg tendencies than from his own personal sartorial eccentricity: "I liked their colored uniforms and feather-tipped caps. I bought one on installments and took part in every parade, marching at a smart gait behind the band." (West, 2012, 32).

Tito learned to speak Czech and German fluently during these early years, and he showed a taste for women which became one of his defining traits for much of the rest of his life.

In 1913, he secured a much better job as a skilled mechanic at the Daimler factory near Vienna, and the Daimler Works soon employed him as a test driver: "The work here interested me more than in any other factory. I even became a test driver, running the big, powerful cars with their heavy brasswork, rubber-bulb horns and outside hand-brakes, to put them through their paces. These were useful experiences." (Dedijer, 1953, 30).

As a subject of the Austro-Hungarian Empire, Tito received his mustering orders later in 1913 at age 21, ending his happy sojourn at Daimler. He asked to be assigned to the 25th Domobran Regiment so that he could receive his orders in Croatian rather than Hungarian. He received specialized training in military skiing, useful in the mountainous Balkans, and, thanks to his continued energy and confidence, he eventually received non-commissioned officer training and the rank of Sergeant Major (Stabsfeldwebel).

In his later reminiscences, Tito claimed that the Austrian army concerned itself mainly with unimportant details, such as learning the names of the royal family or performing intricate drill maneuvers that looked splendid on the parade ground but offered little advantage on the battlefield. While some of this undoubtedly came in hindsight from the perspective of a communist attempting to blacken the reputation of the loathed nobility, Austrian forces in World War I fought with considerably less skill than German soldiers. The Germans showed themselves tough, resourceful men with considerable fighting prowess and high morale, while the Austrian troops panicked more frequently and often fought indifferently.

One curious punishment meted out to soldiers, described by Tito, consisted of capturing a frog and placing it inside a chalk circle on the floor. The soldier was then obliged to keep the frog inside the circle under threat of heavier penalties, for however long his commander decided. Other soldiers might be forced to stand in front of their comrades for hours, loudly repeating "I am stupid, I am stupid."

Tito's NCO rank eventually insulated him from these petty, time-consuming tyrannies, enabling him to study military science, learn skiing on Mount Sljeme, and practicing the role of squad leader. He also learned fencing, deemed appropriate for a "gentleman" – even a sergeant – and claimed to have won first place in competitive regimental fencing matches.

Chapter 2: World War I and Revolution

"Wars of conquest are negative, the subjugation and oppression of other nations is negative, economic exploitation is negative, colonial enslavement is negative, and so on. All these things are accounted negative by Marxism and condemned. All these phenomena of the past can, it is true, be explained, but from our point of view they can never be justified." - Tito

Tito's obligatory military service occurred precisely in time to land him in the thick of World War I. On June 28th, 1914, a Serbian, Gavrilo Princip, shot and killed the heir to the Austrian throne, Archduke Franz Ferdinand, and his wife Sophie, launching the conflict. The Austrian forces entered Serbia, only to be handed several stinging, large-scale defeats by the Serbs. In some of these encounters, largely ignored by later history, the Serbs completely routed whole Austrian armies.

Gallant and fierce as the Serbs showed themselves, numbers eventually told against them, but by that time Russian troops entered the eastern front war in hordes. Tito's regiment found itself deployed to plug a gap left when the Russians fought their way over the Carpathian Mountains to menace Budapest. With the weather already frigid, the Croatian soldiers suffered immensely, dying of cold in considerable numbers. The clothing issued soon fell apart, while the low-quality greatcoats kept out no moisture despite alleged waterproofing.

Nonetheless, Josip noted that the Russians suffered even worse hardships due to equipment inferior even to that of the Austrians. He observed some Russian units with bayonets but no rifles to fix them to. These men charged, unsupported by artillery, in an effort to close to melee range, only to be mowed down by Croatian rifle fire.

During the war, Tito developed something of a knack for leading scouting expeditions and small raids as the lines became relatively fixed over the winter. His platoon slipped past the Russian front lines repeatedly to gather intelligence and spread chaos in the enemy rear. In the course of one expedition, the men surprised 80 Russian soldiers sleeping in a house with no sentries on guard and managed to capture the entire group, shepherding them back to Austrian lines before sunup.

With food rations scarce despite Tito's efforts, the occasional "windfall" of meat became a memorable occasion. Tito later recounted the unusual culinary technique used by one of his men after acquiring a chicken: "My orderly, a Tsigane [...] took the hen and killed it and, after cleaning out the entrails, wrapped it up, feathers and all, in a coat of clay. Then he covered it up in hot ashes. When the clay had been baked as hard as earthenware, he withdrew it from the ashes and struck it with his rifle butt. The clay dropped off with the feathers stuck to it, and what presented itself to our eyes was chicken baked to a tender, tempting brown." (Dedijer, 1953, 34).

As warmer spring weather began to return to the Balkans in the early months of 1915, the Russians renewed their Carpathian offensive, including in the sector held by Tito's regiment. Easter fell on March 22nd, and the regimental officers all left the front lines to celebrate the holiday in whatever style they could manage, but the Russians continued fighting. A Russian attack pushed back an Austrian unit on the Croatians' flank, opening a considerable gap between the two formations. While a Russian infantry unit engaged the Croatian troops in front to keep them occupied a strong force of Circassian cavalry pounced on the undefended gap.

The Circassian lancers in their tall sheepskin hats charged the rear of the Croatians. A slaughter ensued, during which some of the Croatians continued fighting. Others threw down their weapons to surrender, but the Circassians gleefully butchered these men alongside their more pugnacious comrades. Two Circassians attacked Tito, who attempted to fend off one man using his rifle and bayonet. A second lancer rushed him from behind, plunging his spear into Tito's body and narrowly missing his heart. The killing continued until the Russian infantry moved forward and took the remaining men prisoner. The men picked up Tito's unconscious body and carried him with them into captivity. This ended his direct participation in World War I's combat.

Though it proved not to be fatal, Tito's wound took an extended period to heal with essentially pre-modern medical care. The Russians sent him to a hospital in Sviyazhsk, a town in Tatarstan on the banks of the Volga River. Tito remained in the hospital for 13 months, first suffering from his wound, then a crippling case of pneumonia, and finally with typhus caught from infected louse bites. At one point in his delirium, Tito began cursing and swearing at an icon on the wall above him in the fevered belief the painted man was a thief about to steal his clothes. The other prisoners later described these ravings to him. At one point, a nurse tied a red ribbon to his bed to indicate a dying man, but Tito pulled through.

A picture of the Uspensko-Bogorodichny monastery, the site where Broz recovered during the war

Once he recovered enough to shake off his hallucinations, Tito set about learning Russian with the help of books brought to him by two local girls, and by the middle of 1916, Tito had finally recovered enough to start working again. He moved to Ardatov, where a motorized mill existed, and his mechanical skills soon earned him a post maintaining the mill equipment. The mill owner, wanting to retain Tito's services, tried to persuade him to marry one of his daughters, but the Croatian politely refused.

Soon after that, however, the Russians moved Tito again, this time to the Kungur prisoner of war camp near Perm. The prisoners there worked at repairing the Trans-Siberian Railway, and Tito, as an NCO, commanded the other men, all private soldiers. Though the men received payment for their work, the amount proved insufficient to buy warm clothing or sufficient food, so some of the prisoners died on an almost daily basis. Eventually, Red Cross aid packages started arriving, containing much-needed food and clothing. The lot of the prisoners improved briefly as first American Red Cross and then Swedish Red Cross aid reached them. Then the packages tapered off again. Investigating, Tito found out that the Russian section boss sold the parcels after stealing them. He complained to the local Red Cross representative, which stopped the theft but won the hatred of the section boss, whom Tito called "a sinister figure."

The Russian obtained his revenge in early 1917 when several workers stayed in their barracks late to repair their boots. He claimed this indicated Tito falsified everything. A group of Cossacks dragged the Croatian away to the town prison, threw him into the cellar, and beat him savagely with their knouts.

After Tito remained in the prison for several days, however, the February 1917 overthrow of Czar Nicholas II occurred and the Russian Revolution began. The Kungur townspeople stormed the prison to free all prisoners, which allowed Tito to leave and return to the POW camp. A Polish Bolshevik, also freed from prison, had become his friend during their shared time in the jail. The section overseer managed to have Tito returned to the prison after a while, this time for an extended period, but his Polish friend managed to contrive his escape with the help of several other Bolsheviks and arranged for him to flee to St. Petersburg, or Leningrad, where he could hide at the residence of the Pole's son.

Tito continued his adventures through the slowly disintegrating chaos of Imperial Russia's final days. He reached St. Petersburg in summer 1917 during the July Days, when tension between workers and the provisional government reached a flashpoint. 500,000 workers began a series of peaceful demonstrations under Bolshevik leadership, and soldiers dispersed the marches with heavy machine gun fire, mowing down some 700 individuals. A series of arrests followed, temporarily breaking Bolshevik power in the city.

Tito later claimed that he participated in the demonstrations and fled from machine gun fire along with other men. Regardless, police came for the Pole's son, but Tito managed to escape, sleeping under St. Petersburg's bridges for a few days before setting out for the Finnish border. He planned to emigrate to the United States if he could reach Finland, but the border guards caught him and returned him to St. Petersburg. In a radio talk in 1976, Tito revealed his original plan to go to America and added, "Had I done it, I would have become a millionaire." (West, 2012, 44).

Due to his fluent Russian and Slavic appearance, Tito experienced some difficulty persuading the authorities of his identity as an "Austrian" POW and not an escaping Russian revolutionary. The police temporarily imprisoned him in the Peter and Paul Fortress, and even when they finally believed his story, his situation scarcely improved: "The River Neva rose to the very windowpanes. The cell was all stone, and running with rats. Three weeks later I was banished back to Kungur, to the Urals. I was extremely reluctant to return to this place, knowing well that nothing good awaited me there, and I watched for an opportunity to escape from the train." (Dedijer, 1953, 38).

Dmitry Mottl's picture of the Peter and Paul Fortress

Andrew Shiva's aerial photo of the fortress

Tito slipped away from his guards at Ekaterinburg with the simple ruse of asking the man on duty to fetch him water for tea, then merging into the crowd. He traveled on a passenger train, using his fluent, unaccented Russian to inform soldiers who boarded at various stops in search of him that he had seen no Austrian fugitives. Ultimately, Tito rode the train all the way into Siberia, arriving at Atamansky Hutor just as the October Revolution occurred. He identified himself as an Austrian POW with Bolshevik and working class sympathies to the Soviet workers who swarmed onto the train with rifles and pistols. Along with many other foreigners, Tito joined the Red Guard, partly as way to reduce the chances of being shot as a counterrevolutionary spy.

The Soviets provided the Red Guards with weapons, clothing, and food, but they still did not completely trust them. Requests to be sent to the front by the Red Guards met with friendly refusal by the Soviet Russians, who doubtless assumed the men would immediately desert back to the Austro-Hungarian army. Thus, Tito found himself with a detail guarding the Marianovka railway station, deep in east Russia.

In 1918, the situation in Siberia abruptly changed, and it brought important changes in Tito's life as well. In 1917, he met a local girl, the 14 year old Pelageya Belousova, and the two formed a romantic attachment. The following year, one of the Provisional Government's military units, the Czech Corps, began moving towards the west to return to their home country, but an intercepted telegram from Trotsky seemed to indicate their safe conduct through Bolshevik territory might be a sham: "[E]very Czech who is found carrying a weapon anywhere along the route of the railway is to be shot on the spot." (Lincoln, 1999, 94). The Czechs accordingly attacked the nearest Bolsheviks, who happened to be the Red Guards at Marianovka railway station near Omsk, where Tito served. Tito managed to escape the slaughter with the aid of his girlfriend Pelageya Belousova and her family, first hiding with them and then with the nomadic Kirghiz living in the steppes south of Omsk. Tito's luck did not desert him, as the local chieftain, an owner of 2,500 horses named Hadji Isaj Djaksembayev, also owned one of the new mechanical mills with which the Croatian machinist enjoyed great familiarity.

Chapter 3: The Versailles State

"I knew that many things were wrong... I witnessed a great many injustices... But it was my revolutionary duty at the time not to criticize and not to help alien propaganda against [the Soviet Union], for at that time it was the only country where a revolution had been carried out and where Socialism had been built. I considered that propaganda should not be made against that country; that my duty was to make propaganda in my own country for Socialism." - Tito

While the Czechs helped form the Siberian Government and then supported Admiral Alexander Kolchak's short-lived White Russian regime in Omsk, Tito joined fully in the Kirghiz lifestyle. His horsemanship skills enabled him to keep up with his swift-moving hosts, and he enjoyed wolf hunting with them, chasing down the carnivores and spearing them from horseback in defense of the extensive Kirghiz herds. At one point Tito tried raising a pair of wolf cubs, but they decamped to the wilderness as soon as they approached maturity.

Kolchak

The Red and White Russians fought viciously over the Omsk region throughout most of 1919. Finally, the Bolsheviks prevailed, ending Kolchak's reign and eventually his life. With the region back in the hands of the communists, Tito returned to Omsk, suffering robbery by a band of brigands on the way. In Omsk, he found Pelageya, now 16 years old, and married her.

With the Bolsheviks in charge of most of the country, the couple found themselves able to travel by rail to St. Petersburg, now renamed Petrograd. Quarantined in Narva, they eventually boarded the vessel *Lili Feuermann* to sail across the fogbound Baltic Sea to Stettin. Returning to Croatia by train, Tito and Pelageya, the latter now in the late stages of pregnancy, were arrested at the border as communists, but the police soon released them. They finally reached Tito's hometown of Kumrovic in early October 1920.

Tito's homecoming proved depressing. His mother, he discovered, had died in 1918, two years before his return. Meanwhile, his father no longer lived in the family house and now dwelt in

Jastrebarsko on the outskirts of Zagreb. Pelageya soon gave birth to a baby boy, but the child died after two days. Tito, his triumphant homecoming shattered, moved to Zagreb with his wife and found a job at a machine shop.

The Treaty of Versailles, imposing terms on the defeated Germans after World War I, established a large number of new countries out of the old empires. Most of these nations contained a strong ethnic majority, making them potentially stable long-term despite the scornful dismissal of older statesmen who labeled them "Versailles states." However, the Kingdom of the Serbs, Croats, and Slovenes represented something of a multicultural experiment from the first. In the early 1920s, the Serbs supported the creation of a unified Yugoslavia and the Croatians opposed it. The communists also disliked the idea of Yugoslavia, though this would change abruptly within a generation. A Carinthian newspaper seethed, "[T]he leaders of the American Slovenes and the Serbians agree in their demands for a single Yugoslav state. In addition to the agitation in representative bodies there is an insidious propaganda from man to man, woman to woman and even from child to child. At church and at school, the creed of the Yugoslav state is taught and the credulous population swears by its principles." (West, 1994, 48).

Communism took root rapidly in the Kingdom of the Serbs, Croats, and Slovenes. Winning 34% of the vote in Belgrade and 39% in Zagreb, the communists soon found themselves under temporary ban as far as activism went until the government created a new constitution, and in reprisal, a Bosnian communist killed the Minister of the Interior on July 21st, 1921, triggering an even more vigorous crackdown on communism. For his part, Tito delivered a fiery communist speech at the Zagreb Trade Unions meeting in November 1920. His machine shop employer immediately fired him, compelling Tito to move to a small town, Veliko Trojstvo, where his mechanical skills at fixing, maintaining, and operating the local mill outweighed his dangerous political convictions, keeping him employed through 1925.

Pelageya bore child after child, but all of them died from various ailments until the couple's last child together, a boy named Zarko. Tito soon felt confident enough to return to his open communist affiliation, achieving leadership of the Križevci District Committee of the Communist Party in 1924 while continuing to work at the mill.

Tito and his family

After delivering a belligerently communist speech and waving a red flag at a fellow union member's funeral, Tito found himself under arrest, and the police held him for eight days before releasing him. Moreover, the mill owner died in summer of 1925, and his nephew, the new owner, loathed communists. With the police watching him and ransacking his small apartment periodically for communist literature, Tito quit and moved again.

Tito's last job involving physical labor involved repairing torpedo boats in the port town of Kraljevica. He organized a cell of the Communist Party in the town and organized strikes so vigorously that he came to the attention of the Metalworkers' Union and various powerful communist organizations in Zagreb. He returned to the city in early 1927, became the leader of the communist Croatian Regional Committee, and henceforth devoted himself entirely to politics.

The background against which Tito worked witnessed monumental political changes. With the tensions between Serbs, Croatians, Slovenes, and other people who wished to live independently from the others making representative government progressively more difficult in postwar Yugoslavia, King Alexander stepped in, abolishing the Vidovan Constitution in 1929. From then on, he ruled as a "benevolent despot," using royal fiat to impose an uneasy unity on the country. Writing in 1949, the UCLA political science professor and historian Dr. Malbone Graham believed that this approach had worked, abolishing the ethnic and nationalist feelings of the various groups inside Yugoslav borders and making a sort of "de-nationalized," generic citizen: "The old provincial names were wiped out and the new areas were designated by prominent geographical features. […] Thousands of citizens, previously more conscious of provincial loyalties than of the need for national unity, were brought into government […] Finally, distinctions were obliterated between Serbs, Croats, and Slovenes. All became uniformly Yugoslavs, both politically and before the law." (Kerner, 1949, 127).

With the benefit of hindsight, such a view appears utopian and factually incorrect. King Alexander certainly wished to erase the ethnic identities of his subjects, creating an obliging "Yugoslav" whose only identity derived from physical occupation of an area defined solely by lines drawn on a map and a shared central government. Graham thought that the temporary suppression of ethnic identities meant their action dissolution, but events would prove him terribly wrong in the 1980s and 1990s.

King Alexander I of Yugoslavia

At almost the same time the king was asserting his power, Tito busily built his own power using his own arrest and trial as a public venue. In February 1928, he created greater unity within the communist party by calling for an end to factionalism at an important meeting. Becoming the Zagreb Secretary of the Yugoslav Communist Party, Tito leveraged his new position to "advertise" himself, increasing his standing on the global communist scene.

The police first arrested Tito on May Day 1928 when he turned the celebration into a communist demonstration in Zagreb. Released after two weeks in custody, Tito fomented a general strike in response to the June 28th killing of Stjepan Radić, leader of the Croatian Peasant Party. This killing also prompted the dissolution of the constitution by King Alexander and the establishment of the "Kingdom of Yugoslavia" under his personal rule, thus not only bringing Tito to prominence but simultaneously creating the general political structure he would eventually adopt and adapt for his own personal reign.

Stjepan Radić

Tito's mugshot after being arrested

After starting the strike, Tito attempted to hide from the authorities. Police raiding his apartment found a revolver with ammunition, four hand grenades, and a stack of inflammatory communist propaganda ready for distribution that called for the people to take up arms. When the police found him, Tito gave himself a whiff of the romantic fugitive hero by flourishing a second revolver, though he carefully avoided actually using it.

At the time, Tito claimed that the police planted the grenades and revolver, but once in power, he cheerfully admitted they belonged to him. Tito, recognizing the judicial system as a superb political forum in an era of mass communications, made the most of the situation by ostentatiously starting a hunger strike. This earned him international attention thanks to a communist journal, which published the melodramatically titled piece "A Cry from the Hell of Yugoslavia's Prisons" about Tito's sufferings.

Having gained both national and international attention, Tito – much as Adolf Hitler did in the wake of the Beer Hall Putsch – turned the courtroom into a theater, and his presence there into a piece of "performance art." When told to enter his plea, Tito responded with fine rhetorical flourish: "Although I admit the charges of the state prosecutor's indictment, I do not consider myself guilty because I do not accept the jurisdiction of this bourgeois court. [...] I admit that I am a member of the illegal Yugoslav Communist Party. I admit that I have spread communist ideas and propagated communism, that I have expounded the injustices suffered by the proletariat, in public meetings." (Swain, 2011, 12).

Tito received a five-year sentence, but most of it scarcely represented a serious hardship. Due to his mechanical skill, the prison governor put him in charge of running the jail's electrical generators. With his abilities on display, the prison warders soon allowed him to leave the prison and carry out electrical and mechanical work throughout the town; in effect, for most of his sentence, he lived at the prison but worked outside it.

Tito and his mentor Moša Pijade in jail

Released in March 1934, Tito traveled to Moscow in 1935. As he put it, "With what joy I had felt the strength of that country as, emerging from prison in 1934, I listened in the dead of each night to Radio Moscow and heard the clock of the Kremlin tower striking the hours, and the stirring strains of the 'International.'"

Tito headed there because Pelageya had returned to Russia in 1929, after Tito's arrest, taking their son Zarko with her. Filled with communist zeal, she proceeded on to Kazakhstan to teach and to spread the Leninist word, but to Tito's immense astonishment and horror, she had placed

Zarko in an orphanage, and the boy vanished without a trace into the appalling Soviet orphanage system. Tito would not re-establish contact with his son for nine more years, when the young man reappeared in 1944 as a soldier in the Red Army. Tito and Pelageya divorced, and Tito steadfastly refused all her attempts to renew their contact, seemingly still furious over her treatment and losing of Zarko. Stalin's purges did not miss the dedicated communist Pelageya. Sent to prison on some pretext in 1938, she secured her release only 15 years later upon Stalin's death in 1953, after which she lived in Moscow until she died in 1968.

When Tito emerged from prison, Hitler's newly minted Nazi party had achieved power in Germany, quashing the final communist attempts at revolution there. The French communists and fascists continued fighting in Paris and other major cities. The Yugoslav communists now had Milan Gorkic as their leader, appointed by the Comintern. The Comintern weeded out communist leaders they found inadequate with a ruthlessness that echoed the mass "liquidations" of Stalin's 1930s purges. Soon the leading communists grew disillusioned with Milan Gorkic's abilities also.

Gorkic

Unwisely, Gorkic obeyed a July 1937 summons to come to Moscow, and when he arrived there, the NKVD arrested him as a British spy, Stalin's favorite category of imagined bugbears. The Russians shot him on November 1st, 1937, and Gorkic's wife soon faced a firing squad also. Out of 900 Yugoslavian communists then in Russia, the secret police arrested 800, of whom only 40 survived.

After that, the Comintern, threatening to cut off their funding of the CPY, gave Tito command over the party, and the Croatian, then in Paris, returned to Yugoslavia to begin his tenure. Before leaving Paris, he took steps to prove his loyalty to Stalin, including the publication of an article proclaiming, "From hidden Trotskyists you often hear: 'I am not a Trotskyist, but neither am I a Stalinist.' Whoever speaks this way is surely a Trotskyist." (Rogovin, 2009, 308).

Tito began working as effective leader of the CPY, attempting to keep the trust of the Comintern while pursuing his own plans as much as he could. Amid the politics of 1930s communism, Tito soon found himself targeted for elimination by the Paris-based Yugoslavian communist Ivan Maric, who began loudly accusing him of being an imitator of Gorkic, and thus, by implication, a follower of Trotsky and a traitor. However, Tito's efforts in Yugoslavia bolstered his case with Comintern. He managed to infiltrate the legal labor unions in Yugoslavia extensively with communist cells. This led to communist control of most of the country's most powerful unions.

Mustering these results as proof of his true communist credentials, Tito boldly traveled to Paris in June 1938, obtained a visa to Moscow, then went on to present his case. Faced by a series of chimeric accusations, Tito hammered on his very real achievements in creating a burgeoning communist worker's movement in Yugoslavia in just a few months. He also received inadvertent help from Maric, who, panicking, wrote to the Comintern saying that he had no objection to Tito and simply wanted several lower-ranking "Gorkicites" purged from the CPY.

The Comintern worked very slowly on its decision, leaving Tito in Moscow for months. Though Tito, in his later writing and interviews, lamented the bloody destruction of Yugoslavian communists during Stalin's purges, an extensive range of documents in Soviet archives reveal that he played the sinister game to the full. Far from watching as a grieved bystander, Tito ruthlessly denounced numerous other Yugoslavians who might rival or oppose him, deliberately working to bring about their execution. He mastered the fevered "anti-Trotskyist" rhetoric of the show trials and worked pitilessly to cause the deaths of dozens of men and women. Tito also effectively announced his intention to drive out his adversaries in a report made in 1939: "The new leadership stands before the task of purging the party of various factionalists and Trotskyist elements both abroad, and in our nation […] Our party […] will gladly accept any decision which the Comintern makes." (Rogovin, 2009, 308).

Tito returned to Yugoslavia in early 1939 and proceeded to evict his opponents from the CPY. He opposed a Croatian separatist movement which even the Comintern seemed inclined to endorse. Most of the communists wanted to soothe the Croatians' nationalist feelings, concerned that they would turn to Hitler for assistance in creating a breakaway republic precisely as the Slovaks had in Czechoslovakia that year. Tito, however, pushed for Yugoslavian unity and the creation of a revolutionary republic. The Comintern labeled him a possible Trotskyist and summoned him to Moscow that autumn, a near-certain death sentence, but luck favored the Croatian. The Nazis and Soviets concluded the Molotov-Ribbentrop Pact on August 23rd, 1939, one month before Tito's scheduled Moscow appearance. A week later, Germany invaded Poland on September 1st.

When Tito appeared before the Comintern in Moscow on September 26th, his formerly Trotskyist views had now, in dizzying fashion, become the official party line. Prior to August 23rd, Tito's "left-wing communist" views carried an essentially automatic death sentence in Stalin's regimes. Following the Pact's signing, the exact same views became the official line, while the Comintern's earlier view now received the "counterrevolutionary" label. Sheer random chance had saved Tito from "liquidation" by an NKVD death squad. On November 23rd, the Comintern Secretariat put its seal of approval on Tito's approach to a united Yugoslavia and a "revolutionary republic," and confirmed him solidly as CPY leader. Returning to Yugoslavia in 1940, Tito set to work rapidly to build on this base.

Chapter 4: World War II

"The peoples of Yugoslavia do not want Fascism. They do not want a totalitarian regime, they do not want to become slaves of the German and Italian financial oligarchy as they never wanted to become reconciled to the semi-colonial dependence imposed on them by the so-called Western democracies after the first imperialist war." - Tito

Over the course of 1940, Tito swiftly expanded Communist Party of Yugoslavia membership, taking it from 1,500 to 8,000 members. Though still officially illegal, the CPY did achieve some measure of respectability when the older, failing, legal parties applied to it for help and advice. A communique authored by the CPY openly declared its intention to found a communist republic created from a broad-based revolution: "We communists consider that in this final hour it is essential to unite all those forces which are ready to struggle [...] however, we communists further consider that such militant unity will only really bring results when it is achieved not only between leaders but from below, among the depths of the working masses." (Swain, 2011, 29).

Tito sensed that the Germans might eventually invade Yugoslavia, anticipating this event as an opportunity. He planned for strong communist partisan forces to retreat to the mountains, while leaving agents behind in the towns. When the Germans eventually weakened, he thought, the partisans could sweep out of their montane fastnesses and conquer Yugoslavia in the name of Leninist revolution.

In fact, Tito had scarcely laid his plans before Hitler's panzer divisions roared over the Yugoslavian border. Ostensibly assisting the Croatians in their bid for independence, the

Wehrmacht invaded on April 6th, 1941. With typical German speed, the 2nd and 12th Armies crashed through the Yugoslavian defenses, seizing the capital Belgrade by April 13th. The Royal Yugoslav Army surrendered on April 17th, ending official resistance.

In the wake of the Nazi conquest, the old divisions the monarchy attempted to paper over burst out afresh, perhaps strengthened and exaggerated by their brief suppression. The Croatians established the Independent State of Croatia, a curious mix of puppet state and independent ally on the side of the Germans. Intense partisan warfare soon began, launched by the Ustashe, an alliance of Catholic Croatians and Bosniak Muslims determined to drive out or eradicate the Serbs. Even the Germans found themselves somewhat taken aback at the extent of the massacres and violence committed by the Ustashe, with Edmund Glaise-Horstenau reporting that "according to reliable reports from countless German military and civilian observers during the last few weeks, in country and town, the Ustasha have gone raging mad." (West, 1994, 98).

Glaise-Horstenau initially attempted to protect the Serbs to some extent, but with only six battalions of Wehrmacht at his disposal, he could but stop just a small fraction of the violence. This, in turn, kindled an answering aggression in the Serbs, a pugnacious, defiant people throughout all of their history. Soon the Serbian Chetniks opposed the Ustashe, while collaborating to a considerable degree with the Axis forces in many areas. Ante Pavelic, head of the new Croatian state, assured Glaise-Horstenau repeatedly that he would rein in the Ustashe but never did so.

Pavelic and Hitler

Tito proved reluctant to seize the opportunity to become leader of the communist Partisan movement. He had married Herta Haas, his second wife, and did not wish to leave her and his new son. However, by May, events forced him to flee to Belgrade, where the communist leadership had already gone. Tito issued several proclamations, including an upbeat revolutionary document vowing that Yugoslavia would rise and throw off the occupier's yoke in a communist revolution. The killings by the Ustashe, otherwise known as the Black Legion, won him many Serbian recruits, as did oppressive Germanic rule. The various factions quickly mushroomed into armies; by the end of 1941, the Partisans already numbered 80,000 men and women, while the Chetniks fielded 20,000 and the Ustashe 16,000 supplemented by a powerful "Home Guard" of 85,000. All sides would eventually organize their forces into divisions as their numbers continued expanding.

Tito received the post of Commander-in-Chief of the National Liberation Army of Yugoslavia on June 27th, 1941, by decree of the Politboro of the Central Committee of the CPY. Wielding his new authority, Tito began operations almost immediately in Serbia proper. A region of forested hills and tough, fierce people, Serbia seemed an excellent starting point for establishing a Partisan base area. As Tito explained, "While looking over the configuration of the terrains of Serbia, I saw that western Serbia was most suitable for us, for the orientation of our fighting units, for the organisation of our partisan units and for the creation of a certain free territory […] at the beginning we did not believe that we would create a large free territory so soon." (Swain, 2011, 35).

In fact, thanks to large numbers of Wehrmacht troops being withdrawn for participation in Operation Barbarossa, the invasion of the Soviet Union, Tito's initial plan experienced unexpected success. In August and September of 1941, the Partisans managed to seize most of Serbia, enabling Tito to relocate his headquarters to Uzice. A separate July uprising in Montenegro by the region's inhabitants, who lived up to the death-defying reputation their people had won over the centuries, ousted the Italians from much of Montenegro.

The Partisans' success in resisting the Germans and other factions came both from the intense fighting spirit and courage of all the Yugoslav ethnicities and their large stocks of weapons. Sporting and hunting rifles abounded in prewar Yugoslavia, enabling the partisans of all stripes to attack paramilitary and military posts, thereby obtaining further large caches of weapons in the process. Deserting Yugoslav army soldiers also supplied rifles, pistols, hand grenades, machine guns, and ammunition.

On September 19th, Tito met with Chetnik leader Dragoljub Mihailovic, known to his men as "Uncle Draza," a bearded, bespectacled man who would soon become Tito's bitter enemy. The two leaders formed a temporary alliance for the purpose of expanding the "free territory" already won. Tito wanted to go vigorously on the offensive, while Mihailovic urged a more cautious approach to avoid reprisals.

Mihailovic

Galled by the remarkable successes of the Partisans and resistance by numerous small bands of armed men loosely affiliated or unaffiliated with the major movements, the Germans launched the First Anti-Partisan Offensive on September 20th. The Chetniks attacked the Partisans at the same time as they fought the Germans, despite attempts by Tito and Mihailovic to negotiate a truce. The Serbians felt deep and not entirely unwarranted alarm by the fact that the Partisans enforced a monopoly of communist government in Western Serbia, suppressing other parties despite their strong support.

Two German divisions, strengthened by elements of four more and bolstered by two volunteer Serbian units, eventually threw the Partisans and Chetniks out of western Serbia, recapturing

Uzice in the process. Tito himself barely escaped, leaving his headquarters, submachine gun in hand, just 20 minutes before German *Landsers* reached it. Remarking on this event, Tito admitted that "we did not think that the Germans would go through the liberated territory like a knife through butter, we expected steady pressure and that we would be able to hold on for a long time, that we would get more organised and produce more arms." (Swain, 2011, 41).

Tito offered his resignation to the Politboro in case they wanted to hold him responsible for the disaster, but he found himself left in command nevertheless. Mihailovic continued fighting the Germans also, though he observed that Tito's open resistance had indeed triggered several reprisal massacres by the Germans.

During 1942 and 1943, a seesaw battle moved back and forth across the landscape of Yugoslavia, as first the Germans and then the Partisans gained the upper hand. The gleeful ferocity of the Partisans often matched or exceeded that of their opponents, and the British intelligence officers attached to the Yugoslavian forces often found themselves stunned by the bloodthirsty relentlessness and outright cruelty of both their allies and foes. The intense resistance in Yugoslavia troubled the Axis leaders, Mussolini in particular. At the very end 1941, the Duce wrote to the Fuhrer, "Balkans. It is necessary to eliminate all the hotbeds of insurrection before spring. They might cause the broadening of the war in the Balkans. We should pacify Bosnia first, then Serbia and Montenegro. It is necessary for our armed forces to collaborate according to a common plan, in order to avoid a loss of energy and to reach the desired results with the least amount of men and material." (Dedijer, 1953, 184).

Hitler accepted this proposal, and the anti-partisan actions in Yugoslavia developed almost precisely as Mussolini laid out. The Second Anti-Partisan Offensive began in January 1942 and continued through February, evicting the Partisans from Eastern Serbia. The follow-up operation, the Third Anti-Partisan Offensive, aimed not only at Serbia but also at Bosnia, Herzegovina, and Montenegro. During the Third Partisan Offensive, the Germans, Italians, Ustashe, and those Chetniks who now openly cooperated with the invaders in anti-Partisan operations pushed forward slowly against heavy resistance in March 1942. The protracted offensive continued throughout April and into early May.

On May 1st, Tito held the Partisan Olympics at Foca. With the Commander-in-Chief as a spectator, teams from the Supreme HQ, First Proletarian Brigade, and assorted other units contended at volleyball, soccer, and field and track. At this point, the leading Italian units continued their advance just 7 miles distant. After the Olympics, Tito withdrew his five Proletarian Brigades into the mountains between Bosnia and Montenegro, eluding an Axis encirclement attempt. At one point, Tito came across a small abandoned mill and, overtaken by his old obsession, worked for 30 minutes on the mill machinery. Once the mill started working again, Tito and his men moved on.

From there, the Proletarian Brigades and other Partisan units launched a counteroffensive in

Eastern Bosnia. Tito liberated the regional capital Bihac, along with 10 other towns, with 30,000 Partisans installed as a garrison force. Though the Partisans endured numerous hardships campaigning in the rough terrain and wild countryside, they maintained a high esprit de corps, as one account suggests: "After two days of battle, we were tired, dirty and hungry. Passing through a town, the people there ran out onto the streets to wave at and greet us. The battalion commander told one soldier with a strong voice to lead the troops in a song. They sang with him, loudly and clearly. We raised our heads, our exhaustion disappeared and each step became stronger and more resolute. The people watched us and admired us. They said, "There goes the people's army, the Proletarians."' (Vuksic, 2003, 31).

The Germans called this liberated area "Tito's Territory," clearly recognizing the figurehead and mastermind behind the massively successful Partisan movement. Tito, though a communist and therefore officially an atheist, ordered his men to restore the Serbian churches dismantled or decommissioned by the Ustashe. This won him immense popularity among the masses of ordinary Serbs, who provided him with hundreds of thousands of fearlessly aggressive infantry. By late 1942, Tito's Partisans mustered so many men and women that a larger unit – the Corps, consisting of 9 divisions – appeared in the organizational table of the growing army. The Partisans had almost reached the organization and professionalism of a regular army, though they proved just as apt to commit massacres as the Ustashe.

In the beginning of 1943, the Germans and Italians under General Alexander von Leer launched the Fourth Anti-Partisan Offensive, also known as Operation White (*Fall Weiss*). 90,000 men supported by 12 air squadrons participated in the offensive. These included the 7th SS Volunteer Mountain Division *Prinz Eugen* under SS-Gruppenfuhrer Artur Gustav Phleps, and the 369th (Croatian) Infantry Division, known as the "Devil's Division" (Teufels-Division), among others. Marking the unusual nature of the Yugoslavian war, the Chetniks fought alongside the Italians – as allies, rather than servants or collaborators – yet retained a deadly enmity with the Germans. While the Chetniks attacked the communist Partisans, they remained prepared to attack the Germans also, while the German High Command ordered their troops to wipe out the Chetniks if they came in contact with them.

This bizarre mix of enmity and alliance did not flow in only one direction. Tito opened negotiations with the Germans for a time in March, and during that interval, he issued an order to his troops: "On your way, do not fight Germans […] Your most important task at this moment is to annihilate the Chetniks of Draza Mihailovic and to destroy their command apparatus which represents the greatest danger to the development of the National Liberation Struggle."(Roberts, 1987, 102).

With his characteristic audacity and initiative, Tito turned the Fourth Anti-Partisan Offensive into a springboard for a Partisan offensive into Montenegro. The Partisans seized most of Montenegro and smashed the Chetniks as a military force, after which the Germans mopped up their remnants and nearly managed to capture or kill Mihailovic.

1943 witnessed two more offensives against Tito's forces. The Fifth Anti-Partisan Offensive struck at Tito's new "free territories" in Montenegro, using 117,000 men supported by over 300 combat aircraft. Heavy fighting continued for months, during which the Germans killed 7,543 Partisan combatants, suffering 913 KIA and 2,132 MIA (probably KIA, given the universal tendency to take no prisoners). This offensive, Operation Black, nevertheless failed, leaving the Partisans in control of Montenegro.

Tito and Ivan Ribar in 1943

The Sixth Offensive occurred in the east towards the end of the year, aiming at Bosnia.

Consisting of Operation Kugelblitz and Operation Schneesturm (Ball Lightning and Snowstorm), the offensive inflicted heavy losses on the Partisans but failed to break up the structure of their units, thus proving largely futile.

During the harsh fighting in Yugoslavia, Tito developed his own set of military rules, designed to amplify the strengths of his irregular Partisan forces. He always ordered the utmost efforts to be given to care for the wounded. In the event of an enemy offensive, safe evacuation of the wounded took top priority, and, in fact, formed the focus of several major battles during the Fourth and Fifth Offensives. Tito believed this increased the morale of his men, and considering the daring and courage often showed by his Partisans, reality seemingly bore out the concept's validity.

Tito also worked hard to inculcate his soldiers with the idea that being surrounded did not mean their doom. Instead, the Partisans received training to pick a single spot in encircling troops and throw their full weight against it vigorously. This almost always permitted a successful breakout even against superior numbers.

Two other precepts of "Tito-style warfare" included the necessity for officers to undergo the same risks as ordinary soldiers, thus preventing resentment, and rear area spoiling attacks during enemy advances. Any major forward thrust by German, Italian, or Ustashe forces triggered deployment of numerous Partisan raiding parties, who infiltrated the rear of the advancing force. These men and women then did their best to disrupt hostile communications to the utmost, making the advance more difficult and less coordinated.

With the Allies in Italy, just across the Adriatic, and an invasion of Normandy looming (though the extensive British deception plan made the Germans believe Calais the main target), the Germans made a desperate but well-planned effort to eliminate the guiding spirit of the Partisans – Tito himself – in 1944. The year opened with Tito executing another of his key maneuvers – when pushed out of one area by an Axis offensive, immediately and simultaneously launching an offensive into a fresh area to gain new territory. As he described this method, "[W]e must not let the enemy force us by clever tactics onto the defensive. We must make up for the loss of one area by the conquest of a larger and more important area." (Greentree, 2012, 13-14).

Tito and the Partisan Supreme Command in May 1944

This time, however, the Germans clearly identified Tito's strategy. The Abwehr deployed 10 FAT (Frontaufklärungstruppe) intelligence teams, who developed a network of local agents to pin down Tito's location. Finally, the Germans deployed an elite unit of Brandenburger Commandos known as the Benesch Special Unit to track the elusive Partisan Commander-in-Chief down. Disguising themselves as farmers and partisans, these men infiltrated the region where intelligence suggested Tito might be found, near the town of Drvar in a valley of the Dinaric Alps. These daring men, knowing certain death awaited them if captured out of uniform, infiltrated among the equally daring Partisans.

To the particular alarm of Tito's lieutenants, they uncovered and captured a German agent within the Partisan leader's headquarters staff in March 1944. Worse, from their viewpoint, the German managed to escape from the cell where he awaited execution and vanished into the countryside. Tito began using one alpine cave as his HQ and sleeping in another to make his location harder to pin down.

Eventually, the Germans decided to send in a unique unit to kill Tito, the 500th SS Parachute Battalion. Formed mainly of SS men who had been sentenced to a special detention camp for minor disciplinary infractions, the Battalion also included a range of volunteers. These men received training in parachute and glider operations, and soon numbered 1,140, organized into 5 companies. The operation, dubbed Operation Rösselsprung or Knight's Move (a chess term), involved dropping the 500th SS Parachute Battalion directly in the valley near Drvar, following a preparatory Stuka dive-bombing attack. Simultaneously, five motorized columns would converge on the suspected location of Tito's headquarters. Several dozen DFS 230 gliders would provide the means for the 500th's airborne assault.

Tito should have been at Bastasi when the attack came on May 25th, 1944, but he had remained at Drvar due to the fact he celebrated his birthday on that date (rather than the actual date of May 7th). Tito's cave headquarters represented a well-appointed lodging, as a description underlines: "In a natural cleft in the rock three flights of wooden steps led to [...] a natural cave, inside which rooms had been constructed with a veranda in front commanding a fine view across the valley. Great wooden beams supported the construction and inside in Tito's office the walls were lined, and the windows curtained with parachute silk, while a huge British military map of Yugoslavia covered a wall behind his desk." (Greentree, 2012, 30).

Just after sunrise on May 25th, 14 Stuka dive-bombers and a squadron of Italian light bombers attacked suspected Partisan positions in and around Drvar. Immediately after the bombing, a wave of paratroopers from the 500th SS Parachute Battalion landed, followed by the main force in gliders. The Germans landed in a wide arc around Drvar, often very close to their objectives, while more landed on the heights above the town to seal off escape into the forested mountains. A ferocious firefight erupted at the Communist Party Central Committee headquarters, which the Germans mistook for a communications center. The SS men cleared the building after a lethal gun-battle.

The Germans, working efficiently, cleared Drvar of resistance by 9 AM, taking a high number of prisoners. At this point, three captured CV-35 tanks – light Italian designs – counterattacked the Germans with their machine guns. The Germans had no antitank weapons available to counter these small vehicles, which pinned them down for several minutes. SS Oberscharführer Hummel ran to one of the tanks and blocked its vision slit with his camouflage smock. However, a 16-year-old female Partisan, Mika Bosnic, rushed to the tank, and, before the Germans shot her, pulled the smock clear. The tanks soon retreated, presumably having exhausted their machine gun ammunition.

One of the prisoners almost immediately revealed the location of Tito's cave, pointing reflexively to its location when a German showed him the Partisan leader's photograph. Tito soon observed German soldiers closing on the cave across the valley floor. SS machine gun teams set up heavy machine guns, sited to prevent anyone from leaving the cave mouth alive.

Tito, along with the 12 men and 8 women in the cave with him, escaped through the floor. Cutting through the floorboards, they lowered a rope ladder into the stream flowing under part of the HQ. Thick vegetation hid the streambed from observation, and the partisans had earlier placed a rope ladder up the cleft of the falling stream to the plateau above. Tito, his followers, and his Alsatian dog Tiger climbed up to safety. As Tito put it, "I left with the help of my escort and my dog, Tiger. After we climbed for a while, I had to take a rest. Tiger came to me. He started to whine. I grabbed him by the snout to keep him quiet. There were times that I thought we would have to shoot him with a pistol, because he would betray us, but I couldn't bring myself to do it." (Greentree, 2012, 52-53).

With Tito clear, the Partisans mounted increasingly powerful counterattacks against the 500th SS Parachute Battalion, forcing it back into a defensive perimeter. The Germans held out overnight despite constant heavy attacks, with the Partisans drawing off at morning when Luftwaffe air support arrived. Later on May 26th, the German motorized forces arrived, including the feared 7th SS Division "Prinz Eugen." After some additional fighting, the Partisans retreated, as a German officer recounted: "We stormed up the hill and in a single rush, firing from the hip and lobbing hand grenades, we crushed the enemy. The entire regiment […] pursued the enemy as he fled to the north. The latter offered no resistance, because their objective of enabling Tito to escape had been achieved. Tito got away, though […] he had to leave his brand new Marshal's uniform behind." (Kurowski, 2005, 269).

After his escape, Tito allowed the Allies to evacuate him, first by air and then by sea, to the island of Vis in the Adriatic. There he set up his headquarters in another cave. The Germans soon located him there, but the island's defenses proved so formidable that they made no further attempts on the Partisan leader there.

At this moment, politics entered the picture amid the continuing military operations. British Prime Minister Winston Churchill sent Ivan Subasic to Vis, compelling Tito, using the lever of British aid, to nominally accept the legitimacy of King Petar, currently in exile in England. Tito felt rather displeased at this, preferring not to have any dealings with the monarchy due to his communist leanings. Nonetheless, Tito traveled to confer with Winston Churchill in Naples on August 12th. At the meeting, the Partisan leader promised to allow a multi-party democracy in Yugoslavia, essentially promising the Englishman whatever he wanted as long as Allied support for the Yugoslavian Partisans continued.

Tito and Churchill in Italy in 1944

On the night of September 18th to 19th, 1944, Tito slipped off Vis on a journey to Moscow, which he did not warn the British about. In Moscow, he met with Stalin, and Tito took a surprisingly independent tone in his conference with the Soviet strongman, essentially stating that if the Soviets did not assist him, they should at least stand out of his way. Hearing Tito still complaining about King Petar, Stalin offered some avuncular counsel: "You don't have to return him forever. Only for a while, then slip a knife into his back at the opportune moment." (Banac, 1988, 14).

Stalin and Tito agreed that the Soviets would take Belgrade and leave the rest of Yugoslavia's liberation to the Partisans, which is exactly what happened. Except for a Soviet incursion as far as Belgrade, the now gigantic, 800,000-strong Partisan army swept forward on a last offensive in late 1944 and into 1945. Carrying all resistance before them, the Yugoslavian forces smashed the last resistance by May 15th, 1945, a week after V-E Day marked Germany's unconditional surrender. Tito would say of the war, "Our sacrifices are terrible. I can safely say that there is no other part of the world which has been devastated on a vaster scale than Yugoslavia. Every tenth Yugoslav has perished in this struggle in which we were forced to wrest armaments from our enemies, to freeze without clothing, and to die without medication. Nevertheless our optimism and faith have proved justified. The greatest gain of this conflict between democracy and fascism lies in the fact that it has drawn together everything that was good in humanity. The unity of the United States, the Soviet Union and Great Britain is the best guarantee to the peoples of the world that Nazi horrors will never again be repeated."

A celebration held for Tito near the end of the war

Chapter 5: Tito's Yugoslavia

"Comrade Khrushchev often repeats that Socialism cannot be built with American wheat. I think it can be done by anyone who knows how to do it, while a person who doesn't know how to do it cannot build Socialism even with his own wheat. Khrushchev says we live on charity received from the imperialist countries … What moral right have those who attack us to rebuke us about American aid or credits when Khruschev himself has just tried to conclude an economic agreement with America?" - Tito

Following the end of World War II, the Yugoslav Army (formerly the Partisans) executed tens of thousands of their adversaries, including former Chetniks, Ustashe, and others. Mihailovic himself fell into Yugoslavian hands, and the Yugoslavs executed him in 1946. This, of course, also had the fringe benefit of eliminating many people who might have objected strenuously to the establishment of a communist state.

Tito, riding a wave of triumph and military glory, brazenly engineered the takeover of the nation by his party, the People's Front, in late 1945. Though Yugoslavia held elections on November 27th, 1945, Tito loaded the ballot-boxes in his favor by declaring that large lists of people could not vote due to supposed collaboration with the Germans. In fact, the list consisted mostly of people believed to be anti-communist, with no reference in most cases to any real connection with the Germans.

Since he had effectively declared that only Partisans and their known supporters could vote, Tito engineered a 90% victory for the People's Front. With his party now immovably in power, Tito abolished the monarchy just two days after the general election, and King Petar II Karadjordjevic fled to the United States, where he died in 1970.

King Petar II

Initially, Yugoslavia showed itself to be a ferociously Marxist state, with a secret police, purges of dissenters, numerous arrests, and suppression of religion in the name of communist atheism. Catholic Archbishop Alois Stepinac received a prison sentence of 16 years for alleged

Ustashe activity, though the communists steadily reduced his sentence later. The Archbishop's imprisonment caused the Pope to excommunicate Tito.

Tito's communist party also took over most of the major industries immediately. Tito launched a Five-Year Plan for rapid economic expansion. The CPY expropriated huge amounts of private property. Any factory that worked even a single day during the war years received the label of a "collaborating" business and fell to automatic expropriation by the state. Next, Tito's government seized all property and factories belonging to foreigners, including Yugoslav allies such as the British and Soviets.

The First Five-Year Plan rolled an incredible 27% of Yugoslavia's gross national product back into economic development, 92% of it industrial. This outdid the scope of even the Soviet Union's Five-Year Plans, and caused considerable hardship to large sectors of the populace as production of food and consumer goods dropped to build up a stock of capital goods (manufacturing machinery).

Initially, Tito's slightly unique take on Marxism won praise from the Soviets, as a 1947 article indicated: "The concrete embodiment of the ideas of Marxism regarding the unity of the working class with the majority of working people [...] has been most consistently developed in Yugoslavia where the People's Front unites almost seven million people [...] The People's Front [...] is a social-political organisation of the people in which the working class, headed by the Communist Party, plays a leading role." (Swain, 2011, 90).

However, Yugoslavia soon split with Stalin and the USSR due to Tito's maverick leadership. Tito, in a bid to assist a communist revolution in Greece, effectively invaded Albanian territory to protect Greek communist bases there, without first consulting or even informing either Stalin or Albania's leader Enver Hoxha. Though the Soviets eventually outwardly accepted this action, they began pressuring Tito to add Yugoslavia to a planned Balkan Federation. The Federation, under Soviet control, would effectively reduce all of the member countries, Yugoslavia included, to the helpless provinces of what might be called a "greater Soviet empire." An exchange of letters followed, in which Stalin claimed that the Yugoslavian success in World War II stemmed entirely from the Red Army. In fact, this represented a complete falsehood; the Yugoslavian Partisans largely won the war in their own country independently, while most of what aid they did receive came from the British, not the Soviets, whose support always appeared lukewarm.

The communist Cominform convened in Bucharest on June 28th, 1948 and expelled Yugoslavia from its fold. Though it issued an invitation to Tito and his top lieutenants to attend, Tito refused to travel there, noting "if we have to be killed, we'll be killed on our own soil." (Swain, 2011, 96). That was a clear insight, given Stalin's long history of summoning people to areas he controlled in order to have them killed.

Thus, for several months, Yugoslavia existed in a sort of vacuum, with the Soviet Union looming over it in wrath. Tito already looked towards the Americans, perplexed by the entire affair, to save him from the USSR, declaring, "The Americans are not fools. They won't let the Russians reach the Adriatic." (Banac, 1988, 137). This essentially encapsulated Tito's foreign and domestic policy for the rest of his reign as Yugoslavia's dictatorial president – maintaining a species of communist state while relying on tacit Western support to keep the Soviet juggernaut at bay. Edvard Kardelj, Yugoslavia's Foreign Minister, provided a succinct summary of how his nation could maintain itself as an unaligned state between the two vast power blocs of the 20th century, the free world to the west and the communist world to the east, by leveraging the "tendency among the imperialists to exploit the contradictions between the socialist states, very much in the same way as we wish to exploit the internal contradictions of the imperialist system." (Banac, 1988, 138),

Kardelj

The U.S. and England cautiously adopted a "wedge strategy" towards Yugoslavia, supporting it in order to keep it out of the Soviet sphere of influence and put up a roadblock in the way of Stalin's European ambitions. Tito accordingly ceased giving aid to the Greek communist organizations, paid back U.S. Lend-Lease aid, and remunerated English and American people whose property in Yugoslavia had suffered expropriation. Still, the Americans naturally remained cautious of Tito's and Yugoslavia's intentions. They also could not quite decide how to deal with a country that housed a repressive, dictatorial Marxist regime, yet showed strong signs of nationalism and showed itself willing to defy the still-ascendant power of Moscow. As George Frost Kennan, an influential Cold War political strategist, said of Yugoslavia, a "new factor of fundamental and profound significance has been introduced into the world communist movement by the demonstration that the Kremlin can be successfully defied by one of its own minions (Lees, 1997, 54). By 1955, the US government had given Tito more than $1.2 billion in combined economic and military aid. The English also provided assistance, though on a lesser scale due to their waning power.

Tito's regime gradually moved away from a purely communist approach as the pragmatic demands of survival placed effectiveness ahead of ideology. The Yugoslavians tried a three-year trial period of collective farms, or SRZs, after which they asked the peasants if they wished to stay or leave. Flooded with gigantic numbers of requests to leave, Tito and his cabinet decided to return 1.5 million acres of agricultural land to individual peasant family ownership in 1952. Collective farming vanished in most areas by 1953, with a few notable exceptions.

At around the same time, the Yugoslavian state developed one of its other unique characteristics, the principle of self-management. Under this scheme, many factories worked not at the direction of a cumbersome and dangerous central bureaucracy as in the case of the Soviet Union, but by "workers' councils" elected and staffed by the laborers at the factory themselves.

Showing considerable acuity, Tito declared in 1950 that the USSR actually represented a counterrevolutionary state. Stalin, he said, operated the entire Soviet Union as a gigantic capitalist monopoly. His method, he claimed, placed the means of production into the hands of those Marx intended: the workers themselves. When the West invented the term "Titoism" to describe Tito's rule in Yugoslavia, by contrast, Tito claimed that he represented the true Marxist and that Stalin was the "heretic:" "It is simply that we have added nothing to Marxist-Leninist doctrine. [...] Should 'Titoism' become an ideological line, we would become revisionist; we would have renounced Marxism. We are Marxists, I am a Marxist and therefore I cannot be a 'Titoist.' Stalin is the revisionist: it is he who has wandered from the Marxist road. 'Titoism' as a doctrine does not exist." (Dedijer, 1953, 432).

This, of course, represented something of a semantic dodge, unlike Tito's insightful remark that Soviet communism resembled a gigantic monopolistic corporation. Yugoslavia under Tito matched no other state on the planet. Soon, the workers' councils at the factories received permission to make investments and other business decisions, using the funds their efforts earned, independent of state interference, provided that "ownership" remained divided equally between everyone who worked at the factory and decisions occurred by vote rather than "board of directors" fiat.

On the personal scale, Tito's success with women continued. The Yugoslavian leader met a nurse, Jovanka Budisavljevic, after a gall bladder operation and married her in 1951. Jovanka remained married to Tito for the next 29 years until he died, though their relationship broke down to some degree several years before his death. Jovanka lived until 2013, witnessing both the entirety of Tito's reign and the significant events of the post-Tito era.

Dragan Zebeljan's picture of Jovanka

Stalin's death in 1953 while Tito was visiting Britain represented a major change in Soviet leadership. Tito attempted rapprochement with the Soviet Union, only to be largely rebuffed by new Soviet leader Nikita Khrushchev. However, in 1955, Khrushchev visited Belgrade, and, after reaching something of an understanding with Tito, both men signed the Belgrade Declaration. This promulgated an agreement of mutual non-interference, and Khrushchev canceled all of Yugoslavia's debts upon his return to the Soviet Union.

Khrushchev

Tito felt safe enough to visit Moscow in 1956, and Khrushchev and Tito continued their diplomatic dance for the rest of the decade, but Yugoslavia – in the person of its leader – steadfastly refused any agreement that would reduce the country's independence. Tito continued playing the East and West off against each other in order to keep his own country essentially safe from major external interference throughout the 1950s.

Tito continued to enjoy the high life as he aged, living in superbly furnished castles, supplying himself with every luxury, and continuing to pursue women besides his wife Jovanka. However, he also continued to pay attention to running his unusual state and addressing problems as they arose. In the early 1960s, the self-management program ran into problems due to the difficulties of allotting investment funds. Officials managed to take over the distribution of these funds, compromising the independence of many self-managed factories. This led to the production of unnecessary or substandard goods as the officials pursued their own agendas without reference to market demand.

Tito in 1961

At the same time, consumer demand burgeoned as the economy recovered and the self-management program produced genuinely effective economic activity. Tito waffled for some time, apparently trying to coordinate his efforts with Khrushchev, but the latter's fall removed the likelihood of any cooperation between the Yugoslavian and Soviet economies that would not leave Moscow with the whip hand and strip Tito of his independence.

At the Eighth Party Congress in 1965, Tito increased the amount of money that self-managed factories could retain for investment to 70%, up from the current 30%, thus improving the economic position of the workers and attempting to reduce the power of the officials to interfere in the economy's functioning. The bureaucracy naturally resisted this, wishing to retain its control over investment and thus economic planning and activity.

Tito returned to a measure of centralization in the final decade of his life. Though self-management remained a key portion of the Yugoslavian economy, the 1974 Constitution made the state's structure much more hierarchal, giving Tito the power to resist change and try to keep his creation as an unchanging structure for the rest of his life. The Constitution also named Tito president for life in its first article.

Tito continued to enjoy his extravagant lifestyle during the final decade of his life. However, he no longer had the energy of youth and his infinitely complex system began to ossify without his constant tinkering and guidance. The dissident Milovan Djilas noted, "In the late 1960s, Yugoslavia had another chance, the most promising if also the most uncertain, at democratisation … [but by] the early 1970s Tito more firmly than ever held back the movement for change; he forced creative social, national and individual potentialities to revert to the withered ideals of his youth." (Swain, 2011, 189). Nevertheless, Yugoslavia enjoyed nearly first-world standards of living and a unique system of "self-management" that did not match either communist or capitalist designs. Regardless of its flaws and Tito's human failings, Josip Broz had created a relatively prosperous state that remained separate from the problems of other Cold War countries east or west.

Tito died in early 1980 at 88 years of age, killed by gangrene caused by a leg amputation following arterial blockage. An enormous number of heads of state, including 31 presidents and four kings, attended the funeral of the Croatian machinist who had witnessed and participated in the most tumultuous events of the 20th century. In the end, however, Marshal Tito's unified, multicultural Yugoslavia scarcely survived his death itself. The removal of his strong, unifying personality and its emblematic value for the state enabled the "ethnonationalism" of various racial and religious groups to reassert itself. In the course of less than a human generation, Tito's Yugoslavia shattered, first through political disintegration, and later to the sound of rifles and machine guns.

A ferment of political and cultural movements, no longer suppressed by Tito's presence, bubbled to the surface of national life, discrediting almost the entire state apparatus as hopelessly corrupt. Only the army temporarily remained exempt from widespread criticism or attack due to residual feelings of patriotism naturally centering on the institution charged with defending the nation.

By the mid 1980s, regional party organizations wielded more clout than the central party, greatly impeding any weak efforts made towards overall reform. The continuing economic collapse, which had grown extreme enough to prompt creation of large-scale parallel barter and black market economies, poured gunpowder on the already volatile Yugoslavian state. A report drawn up for the central party concluded that "decisions adopted unanimously at the national level are being carried out only half-heartedly [at the republican and provincial levels], and execution is largely limited to those aspects which suit the particular region at the moment." (Ramet, 1996, 12).

As a result, Serbian, Kosovar, Bosnian, Montenegran, Slovenian, Croatian, Macedonian, and other factions soon formed. A more turbulent, critical media arose, while religion reemerged as a factor in both debate and identity.

Though notionally still existing as an entity in 1987, Yugoslavia became a hollow shell within which four states centered on ethnic identity swiftly emerged – the Serbian Republic under the new leadership of Slobodan Miloševic, Macedonia, Croatia, and Slovenia. Though each territory already operated quasi-independently, a flashpoint for conflict lay in Bosnia-Herzegovina, where Yugoslav multiethnic policies created a population in which all ethnicities represented minorities and none possessed the majority needed to create even a pretense of unified government.

Milošević

Accusations flew in all directions. Croats arrested Serbs, Serbs arrested Slovenians, and outrage rose among each group of people. In the meantime, Milošević achieved immense popularity among the Serbs. The ethnic pride of the Serbs and interest in their past found an echo in the other nationalities artificially circumscribed by Yugoslavia's borders. The Slovenians, in particular, manifested vigorous national sentiment, going so far as to create their own Slovenian military units in which only orders given in the Slovenian language would be obeyed.

The reemergence of natural groupings of people based on shared culture, ethnicity, language, and beliefs found expression in many forms. A vigorous renaissance of music, art, and similar cultural activities, each with a culturally unique approach, occurred within Yugoslavia despite the poor economic conditions. One prominent Yugoslav stated that "the Yugoslav idea is starting to become unpopular in Yugoslavia. Nobody wants to be Yugoslav anymore. People want to be Serbian or Croatian or Slovenian. Yugoslavia doesn't mean anything anymore." (Ramet, 1996, 30).

All of the nationalities within Yugoslavia shared one characteristic to some degree: a vital sense of patriotism and independence. The Serbs exhibited it most strongly of all, continuing their long history of defying foreign conquerors despite their tiny numbers, whether those conquerors came from Istanbul, Vienna, or Yugoslavian Belgrade: "[I]f in some respects the Serbs lagged behind their Croat and Slovene brothers across the border, they never lost their love of freedom. All through the centuries of Turkish rule, the spirit of independence was kept alive in the hill country of Serbia by little bands of guerrilla fighters, half brigands and half patriots." (MacLean, 1957, 22).

In fact, all of the nationalities placed within Yugoslavia felt the same desire for independence. The inevitable result of the situation, the Bosnian War and the Yugoslav Wars, represented a period of conflict which established seven successor states to Yugoslavia: Bosnia and Herzegovina, Croatia, Kosovo, Macedonia, Montenegro, Serbia, and Slovenia. The new nations, actually a return to very old identities, still form a loosely related bloc of countries sometimes referred to as the Yugosphere.

Online Resources

Other books about 20th century history by Charles River Editors

Other books about Tito on Amazon

Bibliography

Banac, Ivo. *With Stalin Against Tito: Cominformist Splits in Yugoslav Communism.* Ithaca, 1988.

Dedijer, Vladimir. *Tito.* New York, 1953.

Greentree, David. *Knight's Move: the Hunt for Marshal Tito 1944.* Botley, 2012.

Kerner, Robert J. (editor). *Yugoslavia.* Berkeley, 1949.

Kurowski, Franz. *The Brandenburger Commandos: Germany's Elite Warrior Spies in World War II.* Mechanicsburg, 2005.

Lees, Lorraine M. *Keeping Tito Afloat: The United States, Yugoslavia, and the Cold War.* University Park, 1997.

Lincoln, Bruce W. *Red Victory: A History of the Russian Civil War, 1918-1921.* New York, 1999.

MacLean, Fitzroy. *The Heretic: The Life and Times of Josip Broz-Tito.* New York, 1957.

Ramet, Sabrina Petra. *Balkan Babel: The Disintegration of Yugoslavia from the Death of Tito to Ethnic War.* Boulder, 1996.

Roberts, Walter E. *Tito, Mihailovic, and the Allies, 1941-1945.* Durham, 1987.

Rogovin, Vadim Z. *Stalin's Terror of 1937-1938: Political Genocide in the USSR.* Oak Park, 2009.

Swain, Geoffrey. *Tito: A Biography.* New York, 2011.

Vuksic, Velimir. *Tito's Partisans 1941-45.* Botley, 2003.

West, Richard. *Tito and the Rise and Fall of Yugoslavia.* New York, 1994.

Free Books by Charles River Editors

We have brand new titles available for free most days of the week. To see which of our titles are currently free, click on this link.

Discounted Books by Charles River Editors

We have titles at a discount price of just 99 cents everyday. To see which of our titles are currently 99 cents, click on this link.

Made in the USA
Middletown, DE
22 July 2017